Slithering Snakes

COPPERHEADS

GAIL TERP

BLACK RABBIT BOOKS

Bolt is published by Black Rabbit Books
P.O. Box 3263, Mankato, Minnesota, 56002.
www.blackrabbitbooks.com

Marysa Storm, editor; Grant Gould, designer;
Omay Ayres, photo researcher

Names: Terp, Gail, 1951- author.
Title: Copperheads / by Gail Terp.
Description: Mankato, Minnesota : Black Rabbit Books, [2021] | Series: Bolt. slithering snakes | Includes bibliographical references and index.
Audience: Ages 8-12 | Audience: Grades 4-6 | Summary: "Diagrams, graphs, and fun text help readers explore the habitats, diets, and daily lives of copperheads"– Provided by publisher.
Identifiers: LCCN 2019026729 (print) | LCCN 2019026730 (ebook) | ISBN 9781623102739 (hardcover) | ISBN 9781644663691 (paperback) | ISBN 9781623103675 (ebook)
Subjects: LCSH: Copperhead–Juvenile literature.
Classification: LCC QL666.O69 T47 2021 (print) | LCC QL666.O69 (ebook) | DDC 597.96/3–dc23
LC record available at https://lccn.loc.gov/2019026729
LC ebook record available at https://lccn.loc.gov/2019026730

Special thanks to Jessica McCarthy for her help with this book.

Printed in the United States. 2/20

Image Credits

Age Fotostock: David M. Dennis, 15 (top); Mc Donald Wildlife Ph, 27; Alamy: Andrew DuBois, 8–9; Norman Tomalin, 12–13; Papilio, 15 (btm); bioweb.uwlax.edu: Bioweb, 3; herpsofnc.org: Snakes of North Carolina, 22; iStock: amwu, 10–11; Minden Pictures: Claus Meyer, 26; Pete Oxford, 15 (middle); Todd Pusser, 28; National Geographic Image Collection: Karine Aigner, 4–5; Newscom: James Carmichael Jr/NHPA/Photoshot, Cover; Science Source: ER Degginger, 18 (main); Joe McDonald, 6; Larry L. Miller, 32; Shutterstock: Dennis W Donohue, 22–23; Eric Isselee, 16–17, 18 (silhouettes), 24 (copperhead, mouse, bird), 31; IrinaK, 24 (snake); JIANG HONGYAN, 24 (insect); Jim Cumming, 24 (coyote); Joe Farah, 1; Le Do, 24 (hawk); srelherp.uga.edu: UGA, 20–21
Every effort has been made to contact copyright holders for material reproduced in this book. Any omissions will be rectified in subsequent printings if notice is given to the publisher.

CONTENTS

CHAPTER 1

Copperheads in ACTION

It's night and very dark in the woods. A copperhead hides in the dry leaves. It flicks its forked tongue. In and out, in and out. If **prey** is near, the snake's tongue will find its scent. Pits on the snake's head will notice any heat. Is prey close? Not yet.

Attack!

A mouse scurries toward the copperhead. It doesn't know the snake is there. But the snake sure knows about the mouse. Quickly, the copperhead strikes. Its fangs sink in. **Venom** flows into the mouse. When the mouse is dead, the snake eats it.

Blending In

Copperheads are sneaky snakes. It's easy to see where these **stealthy** hunters get their name. The snakes' heads are the color of copper. Their heavy bodies have light brown skin with dark bands. This coloring helps the snakes blend in with their surroundings.

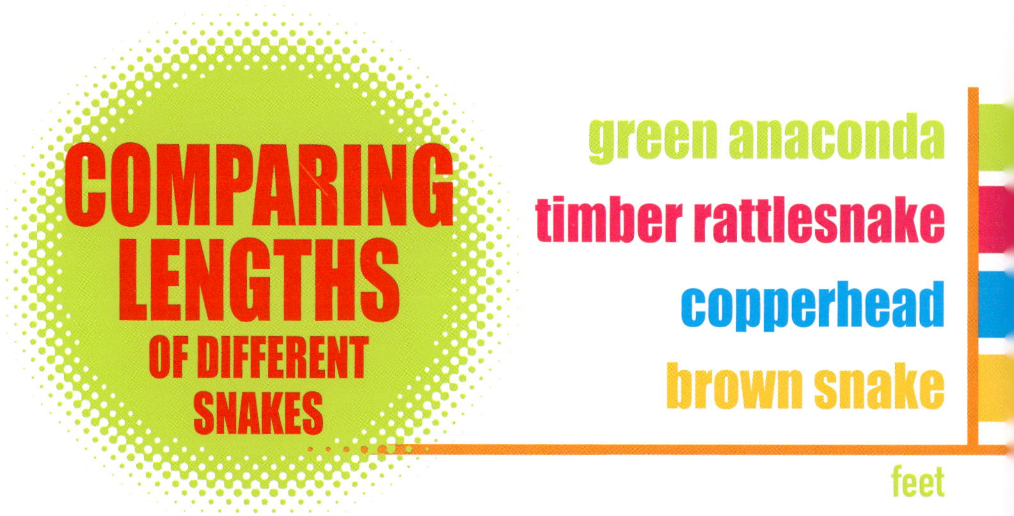

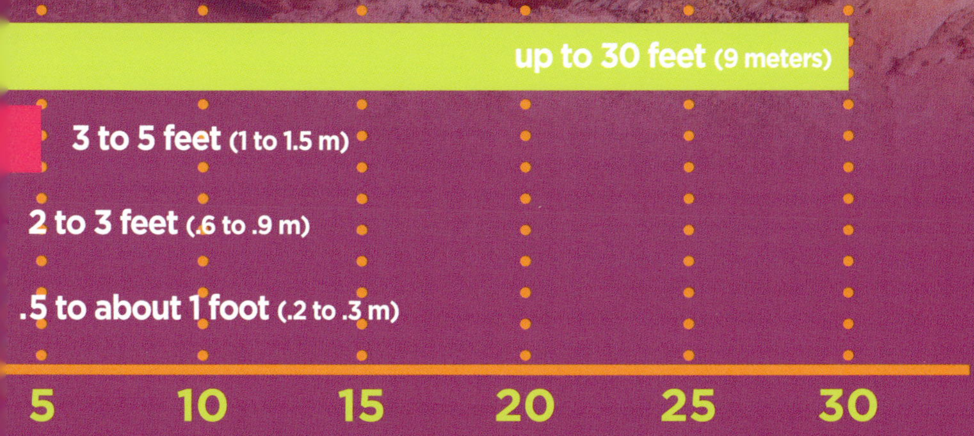

up to 30 feet (9 meters)
3 to 5 feet (1 to 1.5 m)
2 to 3 feet (.6 to .9 m)
.5 to about 1 foot (.2 to .3 m)
5
10
15
20
25
30

COPPERHEAD FEATURES

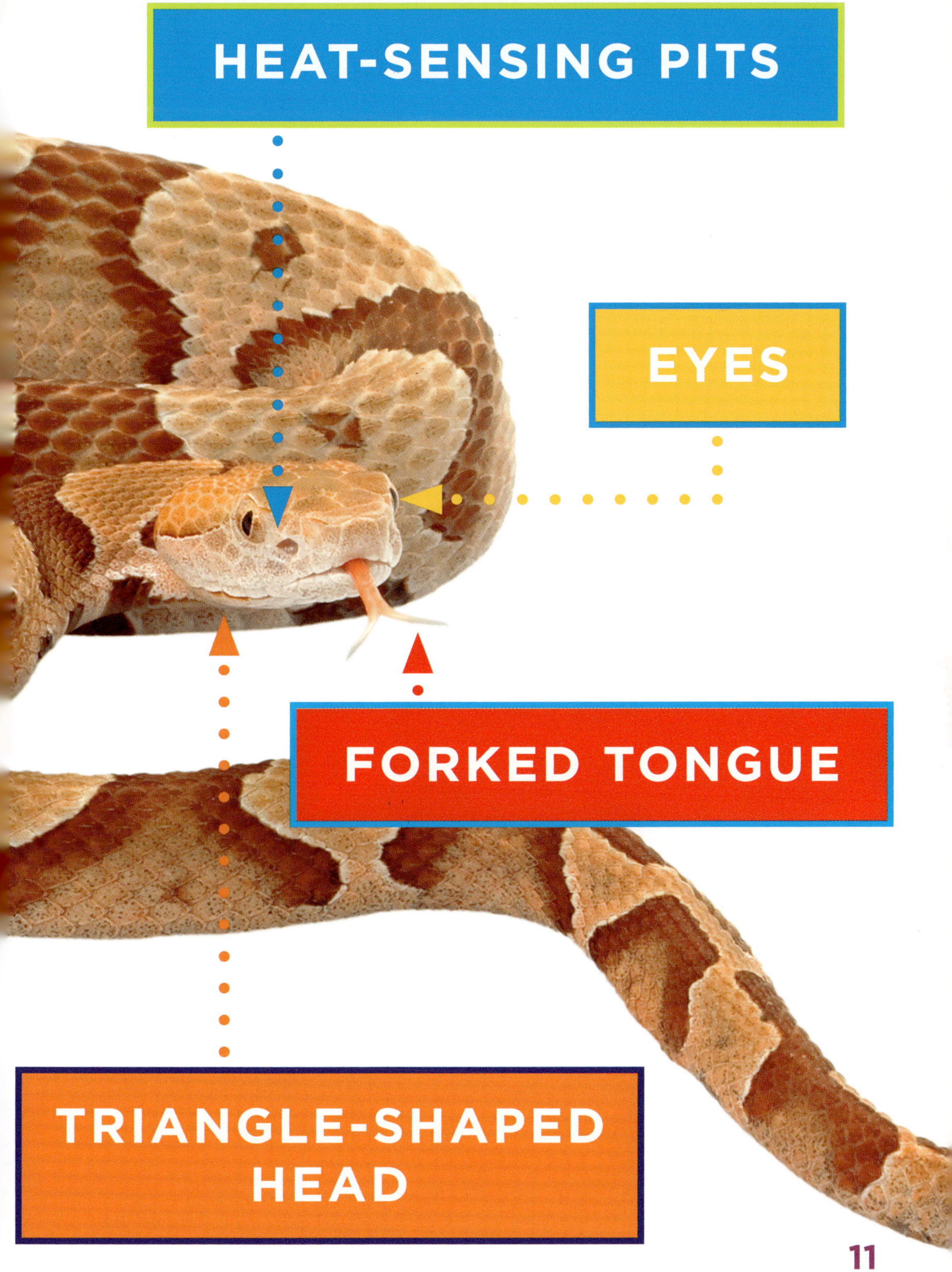
HEAT-SENSING PITS
EYES
FORKED TONGUE
TRIANGLE-SHAPED HEAD

Copperheads are common in the United States. Most reported snakebites in the country are from these snakes. Copperhead venom is fairly weak, though. It hardly ever kills humans.

CHAPTER 2

HUNTING and Homes

Copperheads are ambush hunters. They wait for prey to come to them. Then they attack. They **inject** venom with their fangs. Once the prey dies, the snakes swallow it whole. Insects, birds, and rodents, such as mice, are common prey. Copperheads also eat other snakes.

Where Copperheads Live

Copperheads are found in parts of the United States and Mexico. They live in woodlands and swamps. They also slither around rocky hills and deserts. Some copperheads even live near humans. They eat rodents that live by houses and fields.

As copperheads grow, they outgrow their skin. The snakes grow new skin beneath the old. Then they rub against something hard. The old skin starts peeling. The snakes then wiggle out.

WOODLANDS

SWAMPS

ROCKY HILLS

WHERE COPPERHEADS LIVE

Copperhead Range Map

COMPARING SIZES

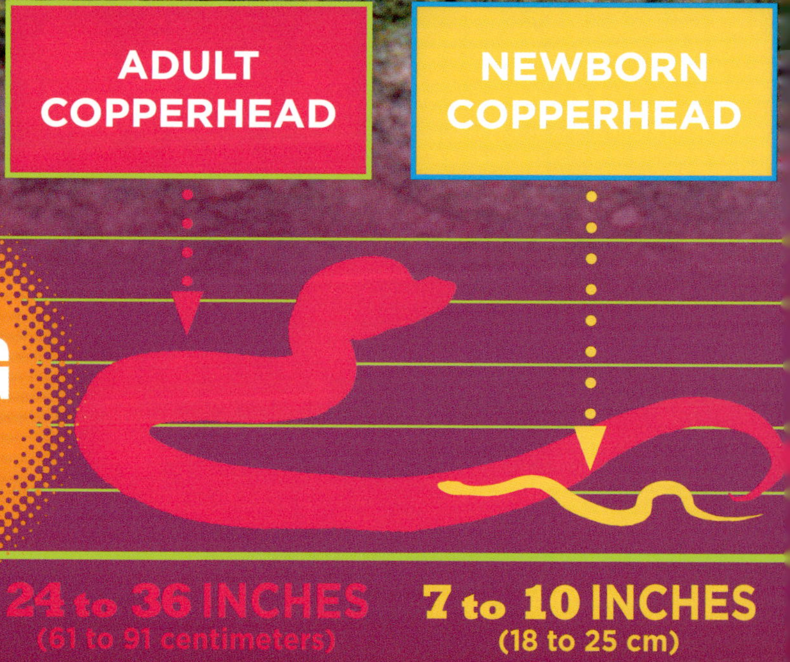

CHAPTER 3

FAMILY Life

Copperheads tend to hunt alone, but they do share their spaces. Males and females **mate** in spring and fall.

Some snakes lay eggs. But female copperheads have eggs that develop into babies inside them. The snakes then give birth to live young. The babies can take care of themselves right away. They have venom, and they know how to use it.

Brumation

In late fall, copperheads usually gather in **dens**. Other types of snakes often join them. They share with rattlesnakes and rat snakes. In the dens, the snakes **brumate** until early spring. They rest through the cold winter.

BY THE NUMBERS

15 to 18 years

LIFE SPAN

about 3 years old

AGE COPPERHEADS CAN HAVE YOUNG

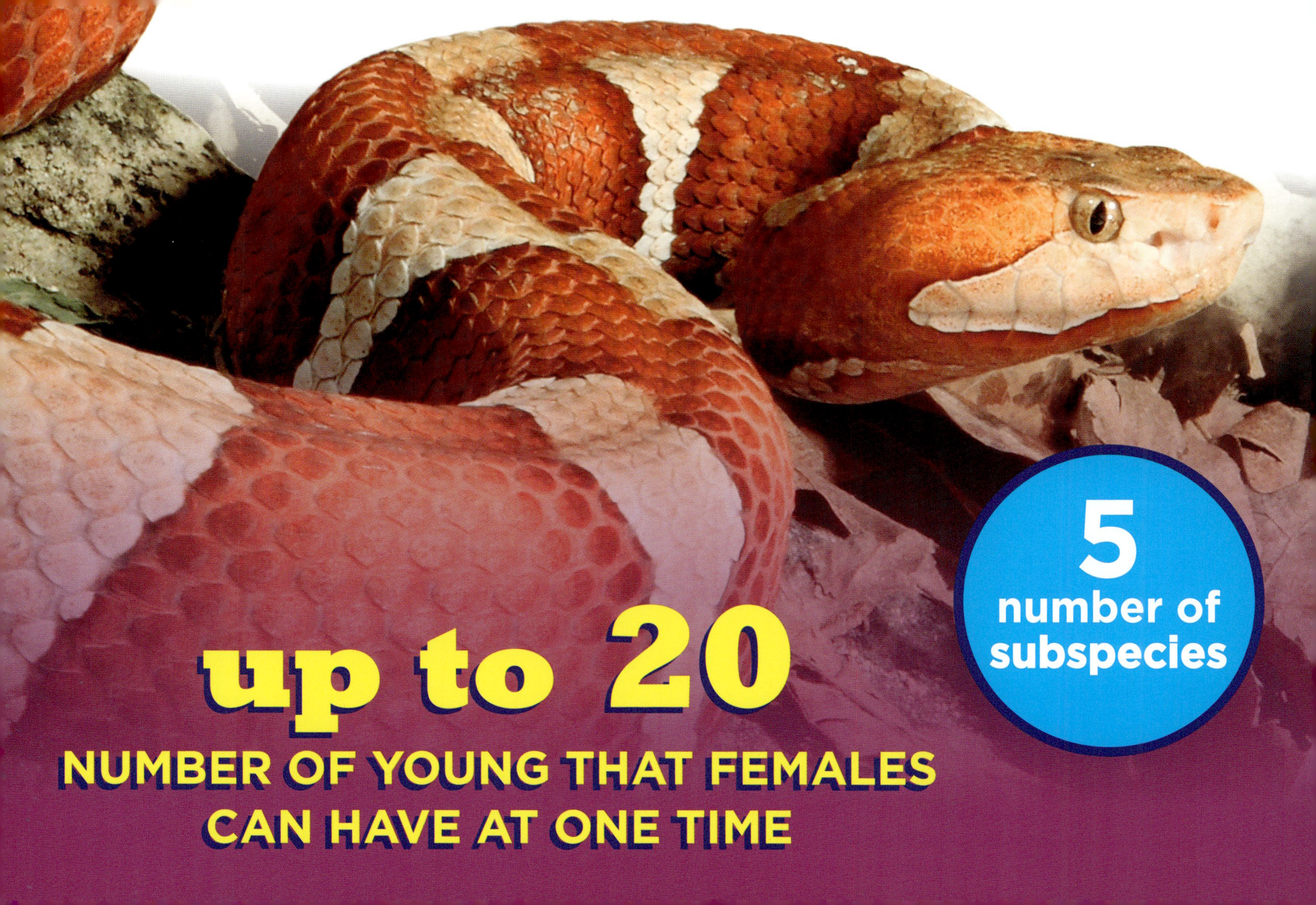

5
number of subspecies

up to 20
NUMBER OF YOUNG THAT FEMALES CAN HAVE AT ONE TIME

Copperhead Food Chain

This food chain shows what eats copperheads. It also shows what copperheads eat.

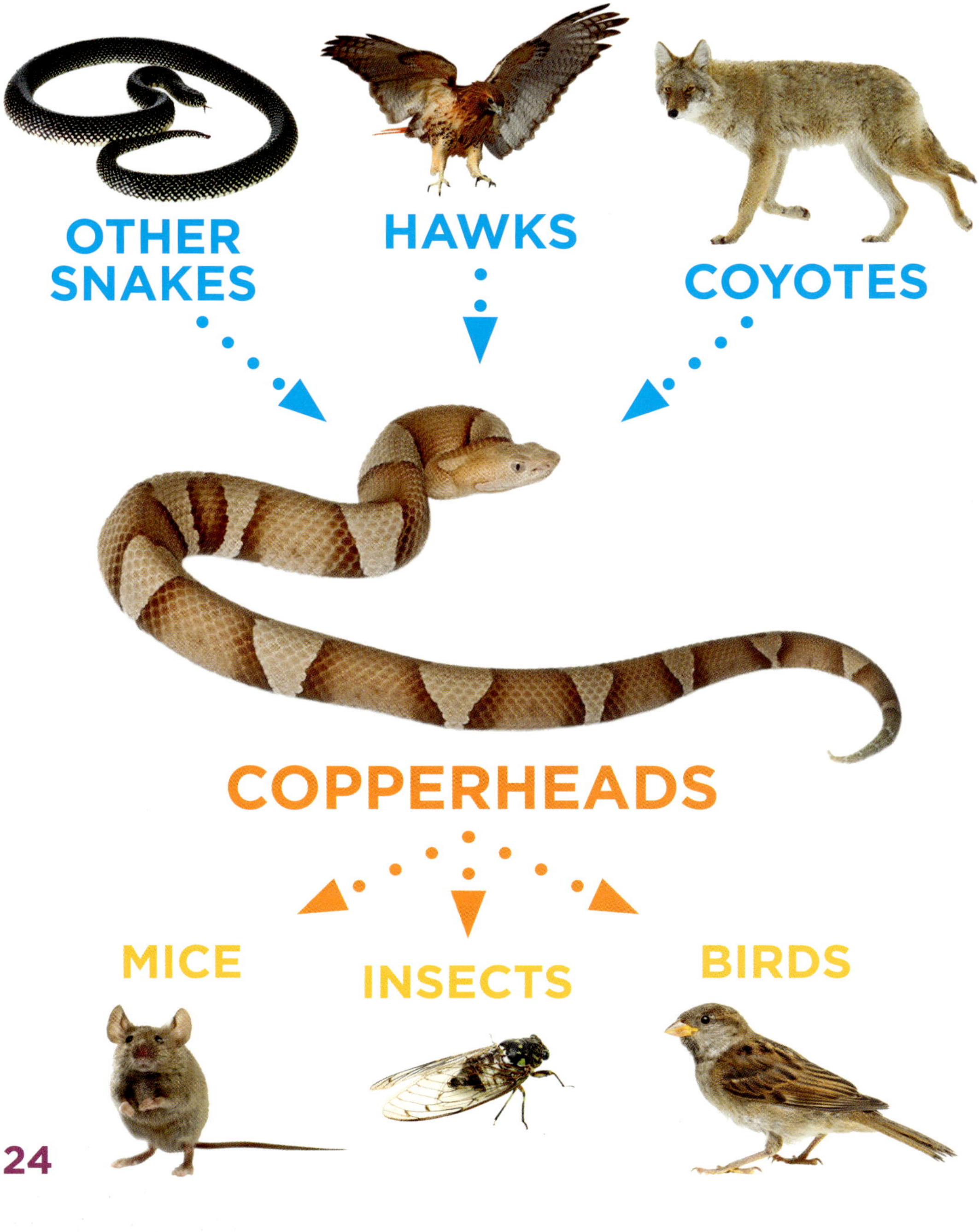

CHAPTER 4

Part of THEIR WORLD

Copperheads become meals for many animals. Large birds, such as hawks, and other snakes eat them. They are also prey to some mammals, such as coyotes.

Humans are also a threat to copperheads. People build where copperheads live. The snakes have less land to call home.

Medical Research

Copperhead venom is dangerous. But it can also be helpful. People have studied the venom. It has a **protein** that helps fight cancer. Someday, it might help slow or stop the growth of cancer.

It’s no problem if a copperhead loses a fang. The snake has backup fangs in its gums to replace it.

A Safe Place to Live

Copperheads are not in danger of disappearing. But humans should still respect and protect them. These snakes play key roles where they live. They're food for many animals. They keep other animal populations in control. These snakes are truly a big part of their world.

Copperheads are protected in several states, such as Missouri and Maryland. It is against the law to kill them.

GLOSSARY

brumate (BREW-mayt)—to spend the winter resting or not moving

den (DEN)—the home of some kinds of wild animals

gum (GUHM)—the flesh at the roots of the teeth

inject (IN-jekt)—to force a liquid into something

mate (MAYT)—to join together to produce young

prey (PRAY)—an animal hunted or killed for food

protein (PROH-teen)—a small material in plant or animal substances

stealthy (STEL-thee)—quiet and secret in order to avoid being noticed

subspecies (SUHB-spee-sheez)—a group of individuals with common characteristics and a shared name that is smaller than a species

venom (VEH-num)—a poison made by animals used to kill or injure

LEARN MORE

BOOKS

Bankston, John. *Copperheads*. All about Snakes. Hallandale, FL: Mitchell Lane Publishers, 2019.

Bodden, Valerie. *Snakes*. Amazing Animals. Mankato, MN: Creative Education, 2020.

Lynch, Seth. *Snakes at the Zoo*. Zoo Animals. New York: Gareth Stevens Publishing, 2020.

WEBSITES

Northern Copperhead
nationalzoo.si.edu/animals/northern-copperhead

Super Snakes
kids.nationalgeographic.com/explore/nature/super-snakes/

What You Need to Know about Copperhead Snakes | Nat Geo Wild
www.youtube.com/watch?v=uqqF-L3O5Lk

INDEX